I0037267

Scan Me! It's Fun

About the Author

Jake is a young Entrepreneur, 6-figure Trader, Trading Educator, Podcaster, Author, and new Father, who, after years of struggling to find that discipline in trading, has now found the secrets that enabled him to reach that highly sought-after accomplishment of 6 figure trader. He has worked tirelessly to get to the position he is in today and is now focused on helping others break that repeating cycle to create the success they are after.

This book was born, through hundreds of hours of research and numerous interviews with 7-figure traders on some of the most common issues traders face today. Through plenty of self-analysis of his journey as well as that of many of his students, Jake was able to put together these 10 steps aimed at helping traders of any skill level.

Originally from the very isolated city of Perth, Western Australia, Jake left a comfortable Engineering job to pursue his passion for travel and exploration. At 25 he packed his bags, and left indefinitely, with the hopes to see all corners of the world, but what he found was worth a lot more than the travel pics. In the hunt for a way to earn while on the go, Jake was introduced to the world of trading and was hooked from the very beginning.

After almost 4 years since his first introduction to trading, Jake can happily say he has found the true freedom that he was originally seeking, it just so happens he found it in an unexpected place. Along his journey, he has faced many ups and downs, and seen a lot of his fellow traders fade away and give up on their pursuit and their dreams. Now he has shifted his focus to providing some of the clearest, step-by-step processes that he feels any new and experienced trader should follow.

The 10 steps outlined in this book really are the basis for all you need for success in trading. Some steps may take more time than others and seem more difficult for some, but work your way through all 10 steps and you will be blown away by your own trading transformation.

Introduction

So you want to become a day trader, but you're not quite sure where to start. I mean the idea sounds great, right? Work from home for an hour or two per day and make an unlimited amount of money? It really does sound like "the dream." But what is the reality? I'm sure you have heard things like "95% of retail traders lose money," or "Day trading is just like gambling." Add to this the thousands of online scams and fake gurus, and it's no wonder you are a little confused. You most likely have one friend telling you to join his $20,000 course and another telling you that "It's super easy! We will just learn from YouTube." Meanwhile, he can't even join you for lunch on the weekend because he has given all his savings to the markets.

Don't worry. I have been there. It is normal to feel a little overwhelmed and confused about where to start, where to put your hard-earned money, and what to expect when taking on this exciting but sometimes challenging journey. I have created this e-book to help you get a head start in your trading journey. Through my interviews and discussions with many 6 and 7-figure traders, and through the experiences I have had throughout my own trading career, I have cultivated a list of 10 steps guaranteed to create long-term profitable traders. These 10 steps are what I would consider the most important aspects a trader must aim to understand on their journey. It does not matter if you have been at this for 5 minutes or 5 years, as these steps range from beginner to advanced, and will act as a guide for you as you progress down the path to successful trading. At each step, you will find a QR code and a link that is aimed at providing you with added material to help with that particular step. I have also added a couple of "BONUS Tips." These are the few things I wish someone told me when I first started. Things I have learnt and incorporated at some point on my own trading journey.

Before we get into the 10 steps, I want to outline a couple of the realities regarding the timelines for becoming a successful trader. What often causes a large amount of disappointment and is the reason for such statistics as "95% of traders lose money", is the difference between expectation and reality.

Here is an example of a very common 'expected' timeline of a new trader.

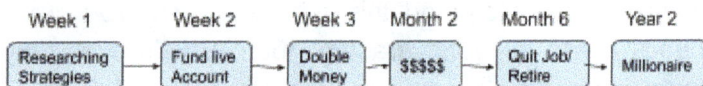

Week 1	Week 2	Week 3	Month 2	Month 6	Year 2
Researching Strategies	Fund live Account	Double Money	$$$$$	Quit Job/ Retire	Millionaire

And here is how that usually plays out.....

Let's take Adam for example.

- Adam hears from a friend how incredible trading is and how easy it is going to be to get extremely rich. Adam has already seen numerous reels and shorts saying the same thing, so he decides to take a deeper look.
- He spends 2-3 hours researching "How to day trade." on Google and YouTube and decides he is going to crush this.
- He spends another 5-10 hours over the next week researching the 'perfect strategy.'
- "Alright, sweet, I think I'm getting this," he says to himself. He has been told by a guru on a free telegram chat that; "Paper trading is a waste of time. All he needs to do is sign up and copy 'these exact trades.'"
- After a few days to a week of figuring out how to connect a broker and 1-2 weeks of research, Adam is ready to trade.
- He thinks to himself, I don't want to spend any money on learning this properly. But I'll happily put this $2k I have saved up over the last six months into my live account.
- **From what I've read, I should be able to double this in the first month. I should have about $10k after 3-4 months, and by the end of the year, I can quit my job, move to a tropical island, and live the rest of my days sipping cocktails on the beach.**
- In his first-week trading, Adam makes a few good trades, almost doubles his money, and

can't believe just how easy trading is. "Sweet, at this rate I'll be quitting my job in 6 months. I LOVE TRADING"

- In week two of trading, he gets overzealous and unfortunately, due to inadequate research, has zero understanding of proper risk management. He takes a few losses, then overleverages, overtrades, and blows his account, wondering what the hell just happened to his dreams of luxury and early retirement.
- He says to himself, "This is a huge scam. This can't be real. I'm never trading again."

The above scenario is a widespread occurrence in trading. It comes from those people who just want to get rich quickly and aren't willing to learn the *ins and outs* that keep them from becoming a statistic.

Don't be like Adam. Do this the right way, and you *will* change your life. Below is a common graphical representation of what happens to the majority of people who get started on this journey.

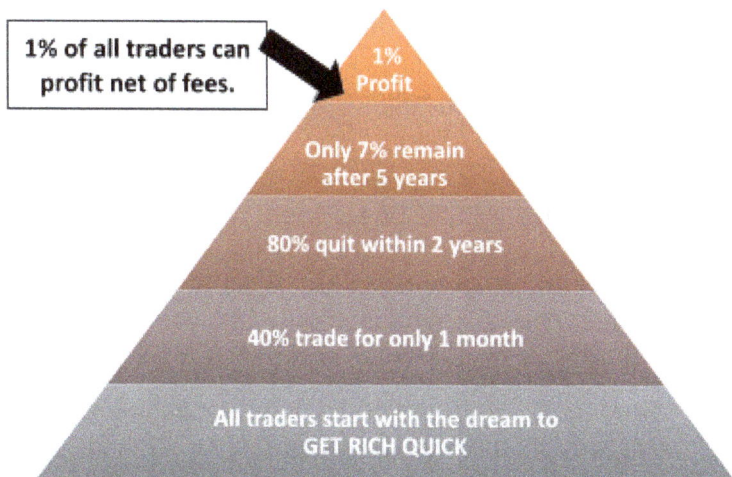

1% of all traders can profit net of fees.

1% Profit

Only 7% remain after 5 years

80% quit within 2 years

40% trade for only 1 month

All traders start with the dream to GET RICH QUICK

So how *do* you work your way up the triangle and make it into the top 1% of traders????

By understanding the **ACTUAL** timeline and following the ten steps outlined in this book. In order to trade successfully and make substantial profits, you need to be 'Ready'. Your environment, your mindset, your strategy, all of it. You need to be ready for the immediate outcomes, and ready for the long-term outcomes. Ready to respond and not react. You need to make sure everything is 'Set.' You must ensure your charts are set up correctly, risk management is set up properly, trading plan, business plan, and exit strategies are set in place, and of course, the correct systems must be set, to ensure disciplined trading psychology. Once this has been done, then the only thing left to do is 'Trade.' If you unlock the secrets within this book, found from interviewing many of the best traders around, I can assure you that you will be completely Set up, and Ready to Trade. Following these 10 steps will allow you to trade with discipline, without emotions, and with high profitability.

Does it seem like a lot? Don't worry, it's not. It really can be as easy as Ready. Set. Trade. Simply follow the 10 steps outlined within the book, and see the results for yourself.

The following 10 steps are presented in order, with step #1 being the first thing you should try to gain an understanding of. As your knowledge grows you can continue to progress through each of the steps. You should keep this e-book with you throughout your trading career as it will act as a guide while you level up to the very top of the trading triangle seen above.

Step 1: What Style of Trader are You?

When we first get into day trading it can be a little overwhelming. At first glance, the charts look like a colorful mess that seems impossible to make sense of; however, this will quickly change. Over the next few months, you will most likely be inundated with different strategies and funky pattern names. You will observe many seemingly strange techniques that people use to better understand what the charts are telling them, and probably be very confused by much of the terminology. It's OK. If you are brand new, I would dedicate the first few months to simply exploring the different possibilities and understanding some of the lingo.

There are many different ways to trade the financial markets. I can tell you straight away that the best strategy to use is the one that suits you and your personality the best. *"But Jake, How do I know which one suits me best*?" The best way to find this out is to simply try them out for a few weeks to a month at a time. I spent the first 18 months of my trading journey bouncing from strategy to strategy in search of that 'Perfect Strategy,' the 'Golden Ticket, much like 'Adam,'' concluding that they were all scams and that none of them worked. The truth is, I wasn't working properly. There are plenty of great ways to take money from the markets, the key is finding one that works for you.

So for Step 1, All I want you to do is find an answer to these two questions.

1) Will you trade using fundamental analysis, technical analysis, or both?

2) Will you be a scalper, intraday trader, or swing trader?

<u>Question 1:</u>

Fundamental Analysis (FA) Trader: These are people who trade based on global economics. These traders will be up to date with current news, and world events, and will trade depending on their prediction of where they believe the economy is going, relative to the instrument they are trading.

Technical Analysis (TA) Trader: These people rely on chart patterns, and repetition in market data to make their predictions. There are hundreds if not thousands of different methods/combinations of technical analysis that people use to create their predictions. You do NOT need to learn them all, just get *really* good at a couple.

<u>Question 2:</u>

Scalper: These traders like to get in and out of the market, very quickly. They will hold trades from as little as one minute up to a few hours. This style of trading can be a little more volatile than the other types. Scalp traders often trade on the 1, 3, 5, 15 minute time frames.

Intraday traders: These traders will aim to be in and out of trades within the day, however, it is not uncommon to be holding trades for a couple of days. These traders will tend to trade on the 15m, 30m, 1hr, and 4hr timeframes.

Swing Traders: These traders tend to catch the bigger moves, and will often stay in trades for multiple days, weeks, or sometimes even months. They will tend to take fewer trades but will have the strength to hold onto their trades despite all the smaller timeframes' ups and downs. Swing traders tend to keep their analysis to the 4hr, 1d, 1w, and 2w timeframes.

Above, you may have noticed that I suggested finding a strategy that matches your personality. This is because your personality is going to have a fairly large influence on your mindset and the way you trade. Of course, nothing is set in stone, and you can always change your style, but knowing this at the start can be a good way to point you in the right direction if you don't already know what style of trader you are. For a bit of fun, you can try a trader's personality quiz. I have provided one from Baby Pips below. A great website full of useful information for beginners.

https://www.babypips.com/learn/forex/which-trading-style-is-best-for-you

Step 2: Finalise Your Edge

As you bounce around from strategy to strategy and person to person, you will find yourself learning a number of different techniques. For example, when learning Technical Analysis you may have heard some of the following:

> Wedge, Flag, Teacup, Pennant, Bullish Engulfing Candle, Bearish Engulfing Candle, Harami Candle, Master Candle, Fibonacci Extension, Fibonacci Retracement, Support, Resistance, Harmonics, Pitchfork, Trendline, EMA, SMA, SMMA, Elliot waves, Wyckoff, M's, W's, V bottom, V top, Morning Star, Evening Star, Doji, Hammer, Haikinashi, Line Chart, etc, etc.

These will most likely all sound like gibberish to you when you begin, but you will come to understand what they mean and represent. While it seems like a lot, I want to give you this crucial tip, again. You do NOT need to know them all, just become *very* good at using a few of them. Most people think that more knowledge means better trading, but this is not necessarily true. So often I see new traders, merging strategies that contradict each other. Unfortunately, you think you are doing the right thing, but without knowing it you are setting yourself up for failure from the get-go. This is the number 1 problem with YouTube University. There is often no structure to the way you learn. As I mentioned earlier, we want our charts 'set' up properly, before we even look at making any trades. Knowing how to do this comes from knowing your edge extremely well.

Find a strategy that matches and works with your answers to step 1. Then master it. Don't worry about all the other *stuff* out there. Most of it tends to become clutter. I repeat, get extremely good at one particular strategy, as that is all you need. Don't merge strategies, and don't try to reinvent the wheel. Find someone, a mentor, or a teacher that you like, and learn every single little detail about the strategy they are teaching. It's recommended to learn live from someone so you can see the strategy in action. Also, try to learn from someone who is having success, with tangible results, it seems obvious, but there is a lot of bullshit out there. A community or trading group is great for this.

You can join our trading community and trade live with us by scanning the QR code below. If you are still trying to finalise your strategy or are unsure where to go to learn more in-depth trading analysis, then we would love to help you out. We have plenty of learning materials and you will be able to directly ask 6 and 7-figure traders while we watch and analyse the markets together.

Step 3: Understand Risk Management

For some CRAZY reason this lesson gets taught at the end of many trading courses, OR not at all, which to me is a HUGE red flag to any trading strategy. Risk management, in my opinion, is the line in the sand that differentiates trading and gambling. You MUST understand that day trading is risky. You have to learn to assess and quantify the risk you are willing to make with each and *every* trade. Understanding risk management is what will keep you trading for the long term. If you are trading with no understanding of risk management, you will most likely end up like Adam. DON'T BE LIKE ADAM.

The key to understanding risk management is to shift your thinking from dollars to percentages. This will also help you later in step 10. It is important to know the relationship between dollars in your trading account and 'Points in *percentage*' (pips) on the chart. The link between these two is 'Lots.' When trading, you will trade in 'Lots.' To make this as easy as possible, I have provided you with the following equation that I use DAILY.

$$Lot\ Size = \frac{(Risk\% \times Account\ Size)}{(100 \times Points\ in\ SL \times Contract\ Size)}$$

As you get more in-depth with your learning, you will get to know these terms, and where to find their values. You may even know them already. At the beginning of this e-book I said you must have your risk management 'Set' before you even think about entering a trade. This is to ensure that regardless of what happens during the trade, you will be able to continue trading for many days to come. For some, this equation can seem like a lot. I also believe it's important to know the process of how I have arrived at this equation. At the Pip Side, we have created a step-by-step system for calculating your risk. I have provided access to the free template below.

https://drive.google.com/file/d/1dJZqr_ALJ30Gd5Cq2dWQqmGT7Pgqj_21/view?usp=drive_link

Step 4: Consistency and Discipline

It's time to tighten things up. By now, you should have a good grasp on the basics of trading and have found a rhythm within the pairs you trade, the time of day, and the days of the week you trade. At this point in your journey, you need to start getting serious and realise that if you want to make a career out of this and trade full-time, you will need to start treating it like you do your job. This means, showing up, every day, on time, and doing what is required.

Consistency and Discipline can be looked at on different levels. Consistency and discipline in; when you trade, and, in how you trade. Step 5 will help us with consistency and discipline in how we trade. For now, if you're not already, I need you to make a decision that you are committing to learning this properly.

You are going to get very consistent and disciplined with a few specialized instruments. First, you need to decide on the pairs you are going to trade, I recommend no more than 5. Personally, I stick to just ONE. Then you need to decide what times, and what days fit into your schedule so that this can become part of your daily habits. It might seem a bit intense at first, but trust me when I say it is worth it in the long run.

If you have listened to my podcast episode with 7-figure trader Teresa Guthrie, you may have heard when we discussed the importance of decisiveness. She attributed her success to a few things, but one most important aspect was her "... absolute, resolute decision, from the very very beginning, that she was going to master this skill set." You may have heard this before, but many highly successful people say that the moment in time when they decide to go 'all in', is usually the turning point in their journey towards success. Let this be yours. I want you to download the following commitment document by scanning the QR Code, insert your information, or better yet, re-write it in your own words. Then place this in your trading space for you to see and read DAILY. This is a major part of the "Ready' section of Ready. Set. Trade.

Bonus hint; Many people use this as the very first page of their trading plan. Look at you go, already onto Step 5. Great work.

https://drive.google.com/file/d/1RiyENCHJe9H-g0-Of2zjZf2XfbZmMkP-/view?usp=drive_link

Step 5: Creating a Trading Plan

As I mentioned in step 4, Creating a Trading Plan will help you with your consistency and discipline in how you take trades, manage trades, and exit trades. From my experience, Step 5 is more often than not, the determining factor between those in the 80% who drop out before two years, and those who are looking to make it into the top percentile. After a couple of years of trading consistently, with a good understanding of risk management, most traders have either found success or reached a level of frustration that forces them to do one of two things. They will either; Quit, or Seek further knowledge on what the professionals are doing that they currently aren't. What they find is .... well, all of the following steps. However, creating a 'Trading Plan' is often the easiest and most natural next step. Moreover, it is probably the most important step that distinguishes a newbie trader from a professional trader. So what is a trading plan, and why is it so important?

Well simply put, a trading plan is a set of predefined rules based on your strategy that you will use to determine whether or not the trade you're about to enter is any good. By analysing your strategy you should be able to find some common scenarios that result in profits, more often than not. By creating this 'Trading Plan,' or 'Set of Rules,' you begin to create consistency in how you enter trades, and (if you have a *good* trading plan) how you manage and exit your trades.

I can not emphasise enough the importance of a trading plan. The monumental changes in my trading journey, occurred when I *finally* let go of my ego and created a trading plan, and it truly was life-changing. However, just creating this trading plan is not enough. You need to create the discipline and mental fortitude to follow these rules exactly as they are laid out. WITHOUT ANY EXCEPTION. For this reason, it is paramount that your trading plan is personalised and thought out in detail. Think of your trading plan as the emotionless version of you, that will help guide you through the emotional turmoil that many newer traders face whilst trading. Because this step is so pivotal, I have created an entire online course that breaks down everything you need in a good trading plan, different ways you can structure it to best suit your personality, as well as some entry-level psychology around how to follow your trading plan, and why some people struggle to do so. You can find the 'Trading Plan Online course' by, you guessed it, scanning the QR code provided.

https://www.pipside.com/the-ultimate-trading-plan

Step 6: Tracking Your Trades

So. How do you know if your trading plan is any good? How do you know what your most profitable trades are? Do you know what pair is your most profitable? Do you know if you trade better with the trend or Counter-trend? Do you know what your most profitable exit is? Do you know your profit factor, win rate, or average R:R?

Depending on your strategy this information can be EXTREMELY valuable in fine-tuning your trading and creating those long-term results. But how do you find this information?

You have to start tracking your trades. At this point, you should be tracking *all* of your trades, objectively reviewing those trades, going over your numbers, and developing those skills to a professional level. If you do not track the trades you are making, how are you meant to know what to adjust? How are you meant to know what is working over time and what isn't? Now, depending on your style, your struggles, and your strategy, will depend on what you are going to track, but the more information you have and the deeper your analytics, the more you will learn about yourself. This is key for the following steps. And yes, I have provided a basic tracking sheet to get you started. Another great tool for gathering analytics on your trading account is to connect your broker to 'myfxbook.' (You can google it.) Here you can get all the information and summation of your trading account. It is unfortunately dependent on your trading platform and broker, which is why I have also provided the tracking sheet for you. https://docs.google.com/spreadsheets/d/1tA_71RD7Nm KB0PLLSO7iSq6uvtVE84ovghMtdDuiEZQ/edit?usp=sh aring

Step 7: Understanding the Role EMOTIONS Play on the Charts

To be perfectly honest, if you have made it past the first two years of trading and you are consistently following your trading plan and tracking your trades, you should already be aware of how emotions affect the charts. Fear and greed are the two major driving forces in all of the global financial markets, and are the basis behind general economics. All of the movement that happens on the charts, at any given moment, is the summation of the total fear and greed of everybody who is placing trades at that particular time.

Below I have attached an image that shows the emotions of a market cycle. It is a very powerful chart and is the stepping stone of your transition from skilled trader to successful trader. This chart, in my opinion, is the 101 of trading psychology. What is Trading Psychology you ask? Trading Psychology is your ticket to the top 1%. Understand this and you will join those who have made a career out of trading. More in Step 8.

Trading Psychology simply refers to the way one's emotions affect the decision-making process, resulting in either the success or failure of a particular trade. The following chart is a great way to gain an understanding of the common behavior of any market cycle. This chart can be used on any instrument and any timeframe. I have attached a link to a video where I go into detail on this topic and show you some real-life examples.

https://youtu.be/f_NQ2John38

WALL ST. CHEAT SHEET™ WE'VE GOT THE WORD ON THE STREET

PSYCHOLOGY OF A MARKET CYCLE

THE FEELINGS APPEARING AS THE MARKET FLUCTUATES.

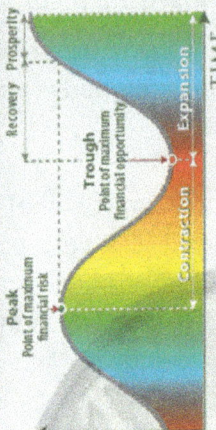

SIMPLIFIED MARKET CYCLE

Peak
Point of maximum financial risk

Trough
Point of maximum financial opportunity

Recovery   Prosperity

Contraction   Expansion

PRICE

TIME

MASHUP SOURCES: BMO NESBITT, BRIAN SHANNON, DR. JEAN PAUL RODRIGUE AT HOFSTRA UNIVERSITY.

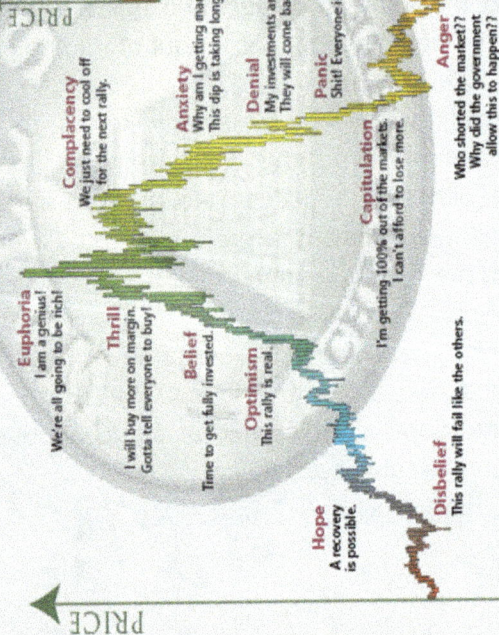

Euphoria
I am a genius!
We're all going to be rich!

Thrill
I will buy more on margin.
Gotta tell everyone to buy!

Belief
Time to get fully invested.

Optimism
This rally is real.

Complacency
We just need to cool off for the next rally.

Anxiety
Why am I getting margin calls?
This dip is taking longer than expected.

Denial
My investments are with great companies.
They will come back.

Panic
Shit! Everyone is selling. I need to get out!

Capitulation
I'm getting 100% out of the markets.
I can't afford to lose more.

Anger
Who shorted the market??
Why did the government allow this to happen??

Disbelief
This is a sucker's rally.

Depression
My retirement money is lost.
How can we pay for all this new stuff?
I am an idiot.

Hope
A recovery is possible.

Disbelief
This rally will fail like the others.

PRICE

TIME

www.wallstcheatsheet.com

WALL ST. CHEAT SHEET™
WE'VE GOT THE WORD ON THE STREET

Step 8: Understanding the Role EMOTIONS Play Within YOU

This right here, is what I believe to be the gateway to the top part of our triangle from the start of this book. Many traders will do all the right things; learn the basics, understand their edge, understand risk management, understand the role emotions play on the charts, have a trading plan, track their trades, routinely and consistently trade, and STILL not have success. But WHY? Why can someone learn so much about trading but still not get the results they desire? Because....

They are not willing to learn themselves. They struggle with the discipline required to follow their trading plan precisely. They are manipulated by the instantaneous movements on the charts. They may track their trades but refuse to spend the time reviewing them or going through their analytics in order to improve. They are unable to control their on-chart behaviors all because they aren't willing to learn the role emotions play *within* them.

Those who break past the '5-year mark', are those who understand the power of introspection and are willing to undergo the personal development required to understand themselves on such a deep level. They desire to learn why and how they behave in certain conditions while trading. This is 'Trading Psychology.'

This is the golden ticket. Once you can unlock the skill of learning yourself, then your limits truly become bound only by your ability to self-discover and grow within. Once you learn yourself, then you are truly 'Ready' for successful trading, and a successful life.

There is a range of different emotions that you will encounter while trading. For example, the four main trading fears. FOMO, Fear of losing, Fear of turning profits into losses, Fear of leaving money on the table. This is just a small example, but the key here is bringing awareness to the more prevalent emotions and THEN doing the personal journey within to understand why these particular emotions affect you in the way that they do. If you went through my trading plan course you would have a basic understanding of just how important trading psychology really is, and how it affects one's ability to follow their trading plan as it's intended.

I can honestly say that 'Mastering Your Mindset in Trading Psychology' is the key to forming those top 1% habits, the difference between following your trading plan and breaking your rules, and the difference between skillful trading and profitable long-term trading. This is the #1 secret you will want to unlock. The Secret of knowing yourself, or better yet, learning how to *learn* about yourself. If you are struggling with any of the above, then you NEED to join my online course, 'Mastering Your Mindset in Trading Psychology'. This course is designed for all traders at any stage and is created as a long-term companion that will guide you throughout your journey. I have designed it to help you understand yourself, provide you with solutions to some of the more common blockages I see in traders, and information on how to track, analyse, and asses your trading, long after you have *'completed'* the course. I truly believe this is the one course that will help you through **all** stages of your trading journey. You can access the course by scanning the QR code below.

https://www.pipside.com/mastering-your-mindset-in-trading-psychology

Step 9: Tracking Your Emotions

If tracking your trades is the key to understanding your trading, then it is clear to me that to understand our *emotions* while trading, we should be tracking them as well.

At this level, we are starting to shift our focus from what happens before the trade to what is happening after we have entered a trade. You need to understand the biological feedback mechanism happening within. First, an action is made (entering a trade), usually on logic-based observations. What follows is the important part. Our response to what we observe during a trade will lead to a number of thought patterns that drive our emotions and behaviors. Once these thoughts are strong enough and/or our emotions are high enough, we will then perform another action, based on the strongest prevailing thoughts. This could be, exiting the trade, trailing stop loss, or entering again and overleveraging based on greed. The list here for emotional trading is endless.

The REAL KEY to success in trading is understanding why you have these thought patterns and learning to manage yourself, and your emotions, so that you only take action based on logical thought patterns (decided by your **trading plan - Step 5**) and not emotion-driven ones. Unfortunately, you can have the best strategy, the best teachers, and the most trading knowledge and still fail. If you aren't able to understand yourself and get down to the core reason you, let's say, flip out as soon as you see red, then you are not going to have the progress that you are striving for.

It's for this reason that I strongly suggest tracking how you are feeling in each section of your trade. I have created an emotional trading journal, cleverly titled "My Emotional Trading Journal," that goes into this in a lot more depth, but in short, I look at trading in 3 phases. Before, during, and after the trade. You may have noticed this in the 'Ultimate Trading Plan' course. If you truly want to understand yourself, it's best to track and journal your emotions throughout each of these three phases, so that you can understand where your emotions are peaking and what exactly is going through your mind while you manage your trades. Once you know what emotions are most prevalent you can begin to work through them. The 'Mastering Your Mindset in Trading Psychology' online course from the previous step is incredible for this.

Once you understand your emotions and have figured out why you are overtrading, revenge trading, trailing too closely, trailing too aggressively, or simply not following your trading plan at all...... then it's time for you to go back and make sure your strategy is still the best it can be. My suggestion is to continuously go back and forth OR better yet, simultaneously track and objectively review both your trades and emotions. You can add columns to your trade tracker from step 6, but often I find traders who have electronic journals leave them in a file deep in the depths of their computers, never to see the light of day. I often talk about how important your environment is for success and thus I always recommend to my traders, that going a little old-fashioned and placing a pen and paper on your desk in front of you, is the best way to ensure you follow through with your intention of tracking your emotions. Buy a book, a notepad, or my favorite option, the emotional trading journal I created, found by scanning the QR code. Then get yourself a fancy pen dedicated to your trade journalling, and even some stickers, for positive reinforcement of the times you traded the way you know you should. These small things *really* do

compound to make a huge difference.
https://www.pipside.com/offers/kobVDmTL

Step 10: The 8th Wonder of the World. Compound Interest

This is the final step for climbing to the top of our triangle. This step is something that can be learnt and implemented at any stage of your trading journey. However, the reason it is last is that, without consistent and disciplined trading, the effects of step 10 will not become present.

To grow our trading accounts to the 6,7 and 8-figure accounts we all desire, we have to be taking advantage of compound interest. What does this mean? How do we do it?

As mentioned earlier we should be looking at our trading in terms of percentage (%), not in terms of dollars ($). If we aim to make 2% of our account each day, rather than $100, then we begin to utilize compound interest. Let's look at the following example.

If you start with $5000 and aim to make $100 per day; After 100 days (assuming you succeed every day) you would end up with $10,000 + your initial $5000 = $15,000. If you aim to make 2% per day for 100 days.

You will start on the first day making $100, but by day 100 you will make $724.46 per day and have an account of $36,223.23. This is $20k+ more than scenario 1, just by switching from dollars to percentages.

Just a quick warning. Understanding this can be very powerful," but with great power comes great responsibility." Often I meet new traders who spend hours looking at daily compound interest calculators, doing the math to find out how quickly they can become a millionaire. "With my $1,250 of life savings, I would only need to make 8% per day for 3 months and I'll be a millionaire." I know this because that's exactly what I did. However, this is the fastest way to become an Adam. DON'T BE LIKE ADAM. To make a higher percentage, we either need to risk more or make more trades. This is not a good thing. **You MUST remain humble, modest, and realistic in your expectations.**

Understand the 'rough' timelines, and understand the process. Create good habits and consistent methods of profitable trading, and allow compound interest to work its magic over time. 1 - 2% a day WILL CHANGE YOUR LIFE. I have provided you with the equation below so you can play around and become aware of exactly what you have in your hands.

$$Acc\ Bal. = Start\ Bal. \times (1 + \frac{\%\ Growth}{100})^{No.\ of\ Days\ Compounded}$$

Lastly, I have included a Compounding Interest tracking sheet. You can put in your information and use it to track your account growth. Simply scan the QR code for access.

https://docs.google.com/spreadsheets/d/1D6Wii06cP7QzDZx4lRi723df8UlfajEWtdseoJGntK8/edit?usp=sharing

Secrets To Success

Now that you have a better understanding of what it takes to become a successful trader, I would like to bring your attention back to the traders' survival rate triangle from the beginning of this book. As you read through this book, you were probably able to relate to a certain number of these steps depending on where you are in your trading journey. Some steps you may have completed, some you may have heard of before and haven't got around to yet, and some you may have heard of but thought, "That's stupid, I don't need to do that." Words I definitely said at the beginning of my journey.

While the common understanding (and teachings) concerning a trader's success is dependent on time, I want to inform you that this is not the case. I believe it is related to how far and how fast you make it through each of the aforementioned steps and how quickly and deep you are willing to go within. However, due to the nature of human learning, it certainly seems that there is an average rate at which we progress, as is seen in the diagram. My goal is to shift your perspective on this and give you the roadmap that will allow you to progress at whichever speed you are capable of, depending on your dedication and ability. With this said, I do not want you to think like Adam. This will take time, but with the right focus, it is possible to bring the 7+ year journey down closer to 3 or 4, with those exceptional learners finding incredible success in just a couple of short years to months (It does happen). All it takes is a decision. A decision of your own dedication, to your own success. (See step 4)

Below I have created four categories of traders and related each one to a level on the triangle. My version of these categories is not based on how long you have been trading but on the number of steps you have completed, as seen below.

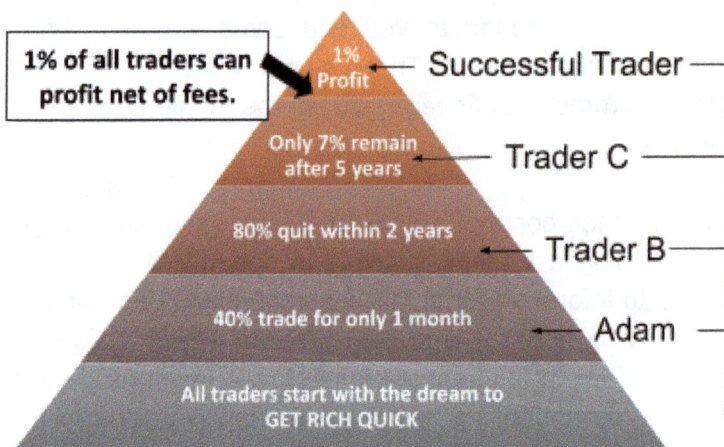

1% of all traders can profit net of fees.

1% Profit — Successful Trader

Only 7% remain after 5 years — Trader C

80% quit within 2 years — Trader B

40% trade for only 1 month — Adam

All traders start with the dream to GET RICH QUICK

Adam:
As we saw at the start of this book, Adams' success in trading was very short-lived. However, Adam actually represents a large majority of people who 'trade'. I refer to this group as the gamblers. People who have entertained the idea of trading and thrown some money

down, without the intention of really trying to learn the skill. They are not 'Ready' they have nothing 'Set' up properly, and they simply jump straight to 'Trade'. Traders in this category will last from 1-5 months. At best these traders will have made it through steps 1 and 2 with a very basic understanding. If they are on the back end of this group they will possibly have heard about step 3 but will struggle to implement it properly or consistently... Don't be an Adam.

Trader B:
These traders have stuck around long enough to truly figure out steps 1 and 2. Most likely the first year was spent bouncing between strategies and styles, but they will have landed on something they like. These traders will have made more of a routine of trading and will have some form of consistency (step 4) although it may be at a base level. Meaning, 'Life' tends to take priority over learning this skill, not the other way around. Most of these traders should understand step 3 (Risk management). However a large majority of them are not putting it into practice, and this is often what leads to their financial losses and ultimately their quitting. The majority of these traders have the basics set up, but they are not truly 'Ready' for long-term success in trading.

Trader C:
Around the two-year mark, those traders who are not yet successful, should have at least settled on their strategy but may still be getting frustrated that they aren't seeing

the progress they would like. At this point, they finally decide they are going to get serious. This is when they ramp things up and properly get into steps 4,5 and 6. By this stage, most traders will have heard the importance of trading psychology or mindset in trading and will have a general knowledge of step 7. Unfortunately, a large number of traders in this category struggle to go any further. Over the next few years, those who do not complete steps 4-6 and at least grasp the concepts of steps 7, 8, and 9, *will* begin to fall away. These traders have understood what it takes, and have completely set themselves up for success, but they are still not ready. They are not ready for proper introspection, change in lifestyle, and a life of freedom. They are not ready for what true, disciplined, successful trading can provide.

PLEASE NOTE: If you feel you are in this category, I can not stress enough, the importance of taking action, NOW. This guide is designed with you in mind. I was stuck here for so long, which is why I have provided you with all the material needed to continue your journey. Please go and scan the QR codes, and set yourself up with everything in this book. Success in trading is 'JUST AROUND THE CORNER'

Successful Trader:
This group of people has worked their way through all 10 steps. They know their strategy, have a trading plan, and are consistently implementing it with the utmost discipline. They are tracking their trades and emotions and were willing to take the deep journey within to learn

what was holding them back and what subconscious beliefs and values they needed to shift to get the success they desired. They have understood the power of compound interest and they have allowed patients to prevail, completely transforming themselves, and their entire lives. This small group of people understood the importance of mindset and were willing to put in the consistent work and personal development that true success requires. This group of people is "Ready". They are "Set," and they "Trade" with incredible success and substantial profits. They have unlocked the secrets and created their own freedom and autonomy. This is your group of people, regardless of where you are now on your journey. You have the roadmap to make it into this group. Follow these steps and you will join those at the top. You will join this group of Successful Traders.

Summary:

So there it is, my 10 steps to becoming a successful trader. Within this book are all the 'secrets' you need to unlock that next level of trading. You should be able to see the importance of each of the 10 steps I have provided and have hopefully gained a better understanding of where you are on your journey. Remember, this doesn't have to take several years, but you will need to go through each of the above steps in order to make it as a professional long-term trader.

Whether you are at step 1 or step 8, I always recommend to EVERYONE that NOW is the time to start growing your mindset. It's time to start learning about trading psychology, as this IS the defining factor between a good trader and a very profitable trader.

If you have gained even the smallest bit of information from this book. I highly recommend you check out our trading community and the lessons/guidance we have to help fast-track you through all these 10 steps. This book has provided you with significant information on what the process is for you to succeed, but whether you *actually* go and do it, is entirely up to you. Now if you are like Adam, you are probably trying to gain as much free information as possible without any intention of investing in yourself. Look, I get it, as that is how I started. In fact, that is the whole reason I created this book. To give everyone a fair chance. However, if you want to speed up your process to success and do this the right way, then join a community, get a mentor, and find an accountability buddy. There is no need to do this alone, and it becomes much easier when you are growing alongside like-minded people aimed at achieving the same goals. We have a free Facebook group. Live community trading, an online trading course, a trading plan course, and a full-length- in-depth mindset course. We even have specifically designed journals to help you track your trades and emotions. Plus, a very specially designed EA helper bot that will truly take your trading to the next level. You can scan the final QR code on the last page, for more information. Now, as promised, here are a couple of BONUS tips for accelerating your journey to becoming a successful trader.

BONUS Tips:

- Don't listen to arrogant traders. **Start in a demo account.** Unless you already have a very good understanding of your strategy and can produce consistent results, or you have plenty of cash to waste, you should start with a demo account. YES, the psychology between paper trading and live trading IS different, but you need to take one step at a time. Starting with real money will cause frustration and create ADAMS. Once you have the basics of a strategy 'down pat', and truly understand proper risk management (Steps 2 and 3), then you can look to trade with real money.

- Read the many books out there that are designed to help you. Learning strategies are important, but so are reading books on trading psychology and mindset. Ex; Market Wizards, Trading in the Zone, Trading Beyond the Matrix, Naked Forex. Etc.

- Link up with other traders so you can learn from each other. Trading is a very individual thing, but trust me when I say, that trading in a group will save you from quitting. Masterminding on the charts and sharing ideas is a great way to speed up your learning.

- Get yourself an accountability buddy who will keep you disciplined and who you can objectively go over your trades with. Accountability buddies are great in all aspects of life, especially when learning to trade. You can even have different accountability buddies for different areas of your life.

- MOST importantly -**GET A MENTOR**
You will save yourself a lot of money in the long run by learning from a professional. The best investment you can make is to invest in yourself. Learn the skill properly. Don't pay to copy trades, get a good understanding of the basics, and get on live trading calls, where you can learn and **ask questions** to professional 6,7,8 figure traders. It doesn't have to blow the bank but investing a little bit in yourself and your learning *will* be worth it. I think anywhere between $500 - $5000 is more than enough to begin. This skill will pay you for a lifetime, and then some. It can create true generational wealth. Learn how to do it from someone who knows what they are doing.

Last Words:

Finally I would like to say this: Learning to trade isn't just a way to earn a bit of extra cash. The opportunities that you can unlock once you have gained the knowledge and ability to day trade are like no other. Not only do you free up a lot of time, but you now have access to an almost unlimited amount of money, and a skill set that no one can take away from you.

Truly understanding these concepts, especially step 10, allows us to take trading from an income source to a vehicle we can use to fulfill any/all of our bigger dreams and aspirations. Once you have mastered this skill, you will truly have financial freedom, and with that, be able to live the life you truly desire.

Trading is *actually* fairly simple. It has 3 basic steps; 1) Learn a strategy that matches your personality and incorporates proper risk management (Steps 1-3). 2) Create a Trading plan around said strategy, that creates consistency and discipline (Steps 4 & 5), and 3) Follow that trading plan EXACTLY as it's written, without any deviation (Steps 6 - 9). That's it. Truly. It really is that simple, however, understanding *yourself* and enduring the hardship and frustration that comes along with learning yourself, is a whole other challenge. It is for this reason that I suggest you take this seriously. Get guidance, learn with others, and from those who are already having success in this. Is it difficult? It can be if you make it so, but is it worth it? YOU BET!! Check out our community, take control of your life, and find the success you deserve.

Scan Me! It's Fun

https://bio.site/TheSuccessfulHippie